Wonder Always Works

A Creative Workbook
On Hearing the Voice of God

By: Courtney Conant & Naci Littlejohn

Illustrated by: Jamie Lyn Wallnau

WWW.WONDERWORKSBOOK.COM

wonderworksbook@gmail.com

Text copyright 2020 by Courtney Conant
and Naci Littlejohn
Artwork and Graphic Design copyright by Jamie Lyn Wallnau

All rights reserved. No part of this book, artwork included may be used or reproduced without written permission of the publisher.

Printed at Hill Print Solutions Dallas, TX

ISBN: 978-0-578-67746-0

EXTRA goodies and TIPS

FOR LITTLE ONES
Go through this book with them! Write their answers and spend time coloring and creating together! You will be amazed at what your little ones hear and see!

FOR OLDER KIDS
Ask! Check in with your child once a week or daily and see what Papa God is showing them! Your excitement will encourage them to keep seeking! Who knows, they may teach you something 😊!

DO THE BOOK YOURSELF
We are all kingdom kiddos! Start at the beginning and go through the activities yourself for an exciting to way to encounter Papa God!

AFTER THE BOOK
...encourage your kids or work together, to create your own Wonder Works activities. Ask Papa God to reveal scripture to you and come up with your own activities to do with Him!

PRACTICE
hearing and seeing Papa God for each other and for other people. The more you practice the easier it will be to incorporate listening to His voice in everything you do!

We would love to see what Papa God is showing you through this book!

FOLLOW US ON INSTAGRAM AND FACEBOOK TO SHARE WHAT YOU ARE SEEING AND HEARING AT @WONDERWORKSBOOK

For another resource in hearing and seeing Papa God, check out Eyes that See and Ears the Hear written by Jennifer Toledo. It changed our lives!

Courtney Conant

In the process of co-writing both Wonder Works books, I have undergone a lot of reflecting about my own childhood, experiencing Papa God's voice, and the purpose behind it all. Growing up, I loved being creative, playing outdoors, writing short stories, and being with friends. It was my dream to one day be a famous news anchor for Good Morning America. I would direct my siblings in "mock" news casts, or set up school to "teach" them their ABC's. I grew up fairly confident in who I was, loved life, and my ability to lead. But somewhere along life's way, through the little things that were said to me, my own poor choices, and life experiences, the reality of my dreams and who I was began to unravel. I found myself all these years later as an adult, a mother, and a wife, broken, lost, and that little girl tucked away somewhere deep inside.

A few years ago, Naci and I read a book called "Eyes that See and Ears that Hear" by Jennifer Toldeo, and I began to experience God as a father and hear Him in new ways. Knowing Papa God's voice changed everything, and I have been trying to listen ever since. You see, not only did His voice begin to uncover and heal the deepest, most broken parts of my soul, but it also revealed the lies I had been believing all my life. The same lies that kept that little girl- full of life and wonder, locked up and hidden away. And as I began to allow Papa God to minister to my heart through His Word and voice, He began to set her free. And here I am all these years later, dreaming again... learning to play again, create again, write again, love life again, and all because I have a good good Father who loved me enough to whisper to my heart and open my ears to truly listen to Him and let Him in. I look at the "kids" (big and small) who enter the doors of our church, or the people I see at Walmart, or at the coffee shop, or on the streets, and I want so badly for them to know they have a Daddy who knows them, and longs to give them life abundantly. I am passionate about teaching His kids of all ages to know His voice so they will never get lost in the lies. To know they can run into the arms of a Father who is real and who longs to whisper His goodness and love over them everyday.

I look at my four beautiful, amazing, wonder-filled children, and I don't ever want them to be hidden. I don't ever want those wild-eyed dreamers to forget who they are and whose they are. I have seen the transformative power of His voice in my own life. It is my prayer and desire, that not only my children, but families and His children around the world, will begin to hear and know Papa God in the realest, deepest way. It was His love and voice that created the world, and we believe that it is His love and voice that will heal it.

May your life be filled with renewed wonder-All my love- Courtney Conant

While writing this book, Courtney and I had an encounter with Papa God. We were in the world and our eyes were opened to the darkness all around. Everywhere we went we were surrounded by millenials, lost children. These children were not prodigals who had walked away from their faith. They were in the world and didn't even know the Kingdom of God existed. Therefore, they were carrying around shame, regret, confusion, lust, perversion, disappointment, sadness, loneliness and pain. Their burdens were the result of a hurting, empty world who does not know its Shepherd or His voice, so they were led astray - seeking to numb their pain and fulfill the emptiness they felt inside.

I share all this because I relate to all we saw. There was a time in my life that I too was in the world living in darkness experiencing these same things but the difference was I knew about the Kingdom, I just didn't know the voice of Papa God. I was following a voice, and I had no idea it was the voice of the enemy. The enemy tricked me into believing the lies he said about me - which affected the decisions I made. It led me to many painful experiences that caused so much regret, loneliness, guilt, and shame.

Thankfully, my story wasn't over. We have a Heavenly Papa who recklessly pursues us! He was pursuing me the whole time...I just didn't recognize Him. All of that led me to co-author our first book Wonder Works - one, to teach my own children how to hear the voice of Papa God, and two, so other families and lost children could learn His voice too.

His voice changes everything. When my ears and heart were opened and I realized all the different ways He speaks, it was like this timeline played in my mind and I began to recognize several times throughout my life that He was speaking to me - I just didn't know it was Him. Papa God didn't wait for me to see or know Him before He started talking to me. He created me, sees me, and knows me, but He also wants me to know Him too. He is always speaking, its just a matter of listening for His voice. When we know His voice, we are led into freedom, and our freedom prepares us to lead others too - out of the darkness into the light!

Love and Blessings,
Naci Littlejohn

a note to PARENTS/GUARDIANS

The ideas for our Wonder Works books were born out of a desire to develop a resource for our own children to start building a deep friendship with Papa God from an early age. We really felt like our kids needed more tangible opportunities at home to practice hearing Papa God's voice, to make scripture come to life, and to develop their own relationship with Papa God through creativity and fun. We wanted to show them that Papa God isn't distant, boring, or just for adults. He can, and does, talk to even the littlest of children and takes great delight in them! What we also discovered after doing the first Wonder Works with our children, is how much we enjoyed doing it as a whole family! We both loved getting to grow together with Papa God as a family unit, and not just as individuals, because that is what Papa God is all about - family! If you choose to adventure with your family through this book, here are a few tips and ideas we've learned along the way:

- Have lots of generous love, patience, and encouragement! Our kids aren't always ready to jump into quiet focused time, (like all kids!) but being loving and patient always went a long way!

- Listen with an open heart, with Holy Spirit, to what your child is hearing or seeing. We found that sometimes (especially our littlest ones) our kids would always hear and say the same thing, or it would seem odd, but what we realized was that Papa God was speaking to them and us, we just needed to keep hearing it! (Example: one daughter kept seeing rainbows and butterflies, over and over, but Papa God kept showing us that He was speaking about promises and new creations!) So keep listening and always ask Holy Spirit for more clarity! Its ok to help them with what they are hearing too!

- You might experience a little warfare, but don't give up! We've had the sweetest times as a family after pressing in and not quitting.

- As parents, we get to show and model for our kids. So, when doing an activity together, we liked taking turns going around sharing what Papa God was speaking to us. One of us would go first to set the tone and to give an example. It has worked well! We found that when asked "Who wants to go first?" that the kids were more open when one of us took the lead and shared. In turn, the kids were then excited and ready to share what they heard.

- Use this as a Bible study. Each of our activities is centered around a specific scripture reference, and we found it was fun and added so much more to our time when we opened the Bible and read more scriptures surrounding or related to the scripture in the activity.

- Most importantly- this time is an invitation to participate and spend time with Papa God and each other. We never wanted our children to feel forced into responding in the activities, but wanted them to desire the interaction and relationship themselves. With a lot of patience and love, we found the more we shared and allowed them space to share they began to want to participate themselves.

Matthew 19:14 "Jesus said, "Let the little children come to me. Don't stop them! For the Kingdom of Heaven belongs to those who are like these children." We hope that you and your family will journey through this book together and discover Papa God through the eyes and heart of a child. It is our greatest desire to restore the awe, the innocence, the spark, the fun, and the wonder of who Papa God really is and His heart for His kids. The Kingdom of Heaven belongs to children and the children at heart. And why?

Because Wonder ALWAYS Works!

START HERE
Kingdom Kiddos

Hello! We are so excited that you have decided to go on this adventure with Papa God! He is excited too because He loves spending time with you! Papa God has so much that He wants to share with you. Before we get started, there are some important things we want you to remember:

1. This is a Special time for you and God. God has many names, you may know him as Lord, Father, Heavenly Father, Jesus, Daddy, King, Savior, and Papa God. We have chosen to call Him "Papa God" for this book, because we hope you get to know him as good daddy! So find a quiet place for just you and Him!

2. Always start by praying and asking the Holy Spirit to come talk with you. The Holy Spirit is the part of Papa God that helps us to see and hear from Him! The Holy Spirit will come be our helper.. all we have to do is ASK Him to come to us!

3. Ok, you might be saying to yourself "You're saying Papa God wants to speak to me But how do I hear Him?!" Well first remember we ask the Holy Spirit to come talk to us, and then we listen. The cool thing about Papa God is that He can speak to us in a lot of different ways. He knows the best way to talk to each one of because He created us!

SO AFTER YOU INVITED HOLY SPIRIT TO COME TALK TO YOU, YOU NEED TO REMEMBER SOMETHING VERY IMPORTANT.

WE HAVE 3 VOICES WE CAN HEAR:

PAPA GOD'S VOICE

His voice is usually the first voice you hear. His voice is always going to speak or show you something that is encouraging, uplifting, and good. Papa God will never tell you anything about someone or yourself that will hurt your heart or be negative or bad. He will always talk to you in a loving, caring way because HE is good and there is nothing bad in Him!

Psalm 33:4 NIV "For the word of the Lord is right and true; he is faithful in all he does."
Psalm 145:17 NIV "The Lord is righteous in all his ways and faithful in all he does"

Example: Throughout the day, you may hear thoughts like..."You can do it!" "You are loved!" "You are smart!"

OUR VOICE

Our voice is our own thoughts and feelings. Our voice is what helps us think and make decisions. It is the voice that makes us different from others by thinking about and helping us decide what we like, what we will say, and what we will choose to believe. Our voice can also make us think that we may not be hearing from God, or it might tell us we are nervous to do what God told us to do. But our voice can also help us to know which voice is God's and which is the devil's!

Example: Throughout the day, you may hear thoughts like..."I can't do it! "This is too hard!" "Do these people like me?" "I look weird!"

SATAN'S VOICE

Satan's voice will always be negative and will lie to us. It will make us feel bad, or make our thoughts feel confused. His voice will try to keep us from doing or hearing what Papa God is saying to us. He is very sneaky because he is a liar and doesn't like anything from Papa God.

John 8: 44 ERV "....There is no truth in him. He is like the lies he tells. Yes, the devil is a liar. He is the father of lies."

Example: Throughout the day, you may hear thoughts like..."Nobody likes you." "You're stupid." "You're not enough." "You don't belong." "You're dumb." "You're ugly." "God won't use you."

DIFFERENT WAYS PAPA GOD SPEAKS

Hearing- This would be the thoughts in our head. As soon as you ask Papa God a question, He will be the first voice or thought you hear.

Seeing/Vision- This is when Papa God will show you a picture. This is like seeing a picture right in front of you or thinking about a picture and imagining it. Sometimes, you may even see a word or phrase in written in your mind too.

Touch- This is when you physically feel Him hold you or touch you. You can also hear Him speak when you touch someone else. Sometimes, when we touch a person (or they touch us) like a hug, or a hand on your shoulder, Papa God will let us feel what they are feeling, like sadness, so that we know how to pray for them.

Feelings/Impressions- This is when you just "feel" or "know" something. You "feel" you should go give your parent a hug, or tell them, "I love you." That's Papa God giving you the impression to do so.

Colors- This is when Papa God shows you a color. Then reveals to you what that color means for you or someone else. He may show you the color purple, and then you see someone wearing purple. He is either "highlighting" (showing) that person to you so you will go share or pray with them. He may also show you purple to remind you of your royalty. Colors have a lot of different meanings in the Bible. If you aren't sure why you saw a certain color, ask Papa God, or find a book or resource that tells you what the colors are for from a Biblical understanding.

Numbers- This is when Papa God speaks to us through signs. You may see the same number over and over. That's Papa God showing you a sign. Again, you can ask Him what that number means, or find a book or resource that has a Biblical understanding of those numbers.

Nature- This is when Papa God speaks to us through the beauty of His creation.

Music/Art- This is when you hear a song and the words speak to your heart, or a song will be in your head and then you will hear it at church or on the radio. Or, He may speak to you while you are creating art.

Dreams- Dreams can be while you're sleeping, or even when you are awake. Pay attention to your dreams, because Papa God may be showing you something.

Others- Papa God can speak to us through other people. An example would be: you may really need to talk to someone and they say just the right thing and you feel so much better! He can also speak through US for someone else, like maybe you felt like just being kind to someone, but that was Papa God speaking to their heart through you!

Scripture- The Bible is Papa God's very own words! Every time you read the Bible you are hearing Him speak! We have picked a scripture for each activity, but you may hear Him tell you to go look up another book and verse for yourself or someone else. The Bible is super powerful because we never have to question if it was from God or true!

It can take a lot of practice to learn which voices you are hearing. Don't get upset or feel like you can't hear if you're having trouble! Just keep practicing! This book will help you learn Papa God's voice! Remember, it's usually the first thought that you hear or see, even if it seems silly! The Bible tells us YOU will hear your Papa's voice because you are HIS! John 10:27 "My sheep hear my voice, and I know them, and they follow me."

HOW TO USE THIS BOOK

4. So what exactly are you going to do in this book? Hebrews 4:12 says that "God's word is alive and working." Papa God's word is the Bible and the cool thing about this book is that it isn't just a book we read, this verse tells us that this book is ALIVE and it is "working" (It DOES something). That means when we read it, we can learn something new from it all the time, we can feel it in us and Papa God uses it to talk to US! There is NO other book that is ALIVE! It's pretty much the coolest book ever!

We want so bad for you to experience how ALIVE the Bible is, so we spent time praying and asking Papa God what verses He wanted to make come to life for YOU. Each page is set up with a scripture (a verse or verses taken from the Bible), and a drawing and activity. We want you to read each verse carefully and the activities. Each page will tell you something different to spend time talking to Papa God about. On some of the pages you might also see a *Challenge* section (it will be marked with a royal crown!). This is really cool because you get an extra activity for you or someone else during these challenges.

When the book is all done, we hope that you don't stop talking to Papa God. We pray that through these pages, you will learn how to take the verses in the Bible and make them come ALIVE on your own!

ALMOST DONE

5. Almost done, but this is really important too. Did you know that Papa God has a sneaky, real enemy named Satan that tries to keep us from spending time with our Daddy? You see Satan doesn't like it when we make time to be with Papa God, and listen to Him. Satan knows how amazing Papa God is and how much He loves His kids. When we spend time building a friendship with Papa God we get to bring heaven to earth and live a life full of happiness and peace, and the devil doesn't want heaven here. John 10:10 says "the thief comes to steal and kill and destroy, but I have come that you may have life and have it abundantly." You see the enemy doesn't want us to have the best life Papa God wants for us. So what do we do about that? YOU get to tell the enemy to leave. If you start feeling like you can't hear Papa God, or you start hearing a voice telling you things that aren't good or make you feel bad you just say out loud "Satan you leave me alone! I ask for Papa God's protection, and you have to GO!"

AND GUESS WHAT? HE HAS TO LEAVE!

6. Last thing, but the MOST IMPORTANT... HAVE FUN!!!! Grab your favorite pens, markers, colored pencils, etc. something yummy to eat or drink, and enjoy spending time with your Papa! Color, doodle, write, make these pages yours! We have prayed just for YOU and know that He will show you really cool things. We hope that He becomes your best friend!

ARE YOU READY?!

ACTIVITY

Jesus explained, "I am the way, I am the truth, and I am the life. No one comes next to the Father except through union with me. To know me is to know my Father too. And from now on you will realize that you have seen Him and experienced Him."

John 14:6-7 TPT

"For this is how much God loved the world— He gave His one and only unique Son as a gift. So now everyone who believes in Him will never perish but experience everlasting life."

John 3:16 TPT

WHEN GOD CREATED THE WORLD, HE CREATED A GARDEN WHERE EVERYTHING IN IT WAS PERFECT AND BEAUTIFUL, BUT HIS MOST PRECIOUS CREATION WAS US, HIS CHILDREN. DID YOU KNOW THAT?! HE CREATED YOU AND YOU ARE HIS MOST PRECIOUS, LOVED CREATION! BUT, DOES THIS WORLD AROUND YOU LOOK LIKE A PERFECT GARDEN? NO! BECAUSE PAPA GOD HAS AN ENEMY, SATAN, WHO BRINGS DEATH, SIN, SICKNESS, AND DESTRUCTION. THAT SNEAKY SATAN LIES TO US AND TRIES TO MAKE US FORGET WHERE WE CAME FROM AND WHO OUR FATHER IS. ALL THESE LIES CAN MAKE US BELIEVE THAT WE HAVE TO LIVE SATAN'S WAY...AND THAT'S JUST NOT TRUE! BUT, THERE IS GOOD NEWS: PAPA GOD NEVER WANTED FOR US TO LIVE IN A WORLD LIKE THAT - HE ALWAYS WANTED TO BE OUR FATHER AND LIVE WITH US HAPPILY EVER AFTER AS A FAMILY IN PEACE, JOY AND LOVE! SO, HE KNEW HE HAD TO DO SOMETHING ABOUT SATAN'S DESTRUCTION TO BRING US BACK TO THE WAY HE CREATED EVERYTHING. AND YOU KNOW WHAT HE DID? PAPA GOD LOVED US SO MUCH, THAT HE GAVE HIS ONE AND ONLY SON, JESUS, TO DIE FOR US. WHEN JESUS DIED, HE TOOK ON ALL THAT DEATH, SICKNESS, SIN AND DARKNESS ONTO HIMSELF AND DEFEATED SATAN! BUT JESUS DIDN'T STAY DEAD, HE CAME BACK TO LIFE SO THAT WHOEVER BELIEVES IN HIM WILL BE SET FREE AND GET TO LIVE WITH PAPA GOD AGAIN FOREVER! WOULD YOU LIKE TO WALK WITH PAPA GOD, AND BE FREE, THE WAY YOU WERE MEANT TO BE? ALL YOU HAVE TO DO IS ASK! YOU CAN ASK BY TALKING TO JESUS THROUGH THIS PRAYER:

Jesus,
I believe that you are the son of God, and that you came to set me free. I believe that you came, died, rose again, and defeated Satan, death, sickness, and sin. I ask that you would come live in my heart, come and make it brand new, and that your Holy Spirit would be my guide. I'm so excited to get to know you! In Your name, I pray, Amen!

WELCOME TO THE FAMILY! LUKE 15:7 SAYS THAT ALL OF HEAVEN IS CELEBRATING YOU! CLOSE YOUR EYES AND IMAGINE YOUR FATHER, PAPA GOD, STANDING IN FRONT OF YOU WITH HIS ARMS WIDE OPEN. HE IS WAITING TO WELCOME YOU INTO HIS GREAT LOVE. AS YOU WALK TOWARDS HIM, WHAT DO YOU SEE? WHAT DO YOU FEEL? WHAT IS HE SAYING TO YOU? IS THERE ANYTHING YOU WANT TO SAY TO HIM? TELL HIM!! WRITE OR DRAW WHAT YOU EXPERIENCE IN YOUR WELCOME HOME PARTY!

WELCOME HOME

ACTIVITY
"NEW CREATION"

"This means that anyone who belongs to Christ has become a new person. The old life is gone; a new life has begun!"

2 CORINTHIANS 5:17 NLT

Now that you believe in Jesus, and have asked Him to live in your heart, you have been made brand new! The old things you have done or said, or struggled with, are no longer a part of you because the Holy Spirit lives in you!

It's like you were a little wiggly caterpillar, but then Papa God transformed you into a beautiful butterfly! You were always made to be a beautiful creation of Papa God! As you decorate the butterflies, spend time thanking Papa God for making you new! Say, "Papa God, will you please show me all the ways you have made me brand new?"

Now take what you heard or saw and write it in the clouds!

ACTIVITY

HIDDEN TREASURE

"Heaven's kingdom realm can be illustrated like this: "A person discovered that there was hidden treasure in a field. Upon finding it, he hid it again. Because of uncovering such treasure, he was overjoyed and sold all that he possessed to buy the entire field just so he could have the treasure. "Heaven's kingdom realm is also like a jewel merchant in search of rare pearls."

Matthew 13:44-45 TPT

JESUS LOVED SHARING STORIES WITH PEOPLE TO TEACH THEM DEEPER MEANING. THIS STORY MIGHT SOUND A LITTLE CONFUSING TO YOU AT FIRST, BUT JESUS WAS ACTUALLY SHARING HIS STORY OF WHAT HE DID FOR YOU, AND HIS LOVE FOR YOU! YOU SEE, JESUS WAS LIKE THE MAN WHO DISCOVERED A GREAT TREASURE! AND WHEN HE DID, HE LEFT HIS HEAVENLY THRONE, CAME TO EARTH, GAVE UP EVERYTHING HE HAD, AND EVEN DIED FOR THE TREASURE BECAUSE IT WAS THAT VALUABLE. DO YOU KNOW WHAT THE TREASURE WAS? IT WAS YOU! YOU ARE HIS MOST PRECIOUS TREASURE! YOUR WORTH IS NOT DETERMINED BY PEOPLE'S OPINIONS OR YOUR CHOICES. YOUR WORTH IS IN JESUS ALONE! AND HE CALLS YOU WORTHY NO MATTER WHAT! SPEND TIME DECORATING THE TREASURE BOX WITH PAPA GOD AND FEEL HOW SPECIAL YOU ARE TO HIM. LEAVE THE INSIDE EMPTY FOR THE NEXT ACTIVITY!

JESUS IS ALSO OUR TREASURE. CLOSE YOUR EYES, HOLD OUT YOUR HANDS, AND PICTURE JESUS HANDING YOU A TREASURE BOX. OPEN THE BOX AND ASK, "HOLY SPIRIT, WILL YOU SHOW ME HOW JESUS IS A TREASURE TO ME?" DRAW OR WRITE WHAT HE SHOWED YOU INSIDE THE TREASURE BOX.

ACTIVITY 4
WE ALL FIT TOGETHER

"A person has only one body, but it has many parts. Yes, there are many parts, but all those parts are still just one body. Christ is like that too...But as it is, God put the parts in the body as he wanted them. He made a place for each one. So there are many parts, but only one body."

1 Corinthians 12:12;14 ERV

WHEN YOU BECOME A PART OF PAPA GOD'S FAMILY, YOU BECOME A PART OF WHAT IS CALLED THE "BODY OF CHRIST." THE BODY OF CHRIST IS MADE UP OF ALL THE DIFFERENT PEOPLE IN HIS FAMILY. IT MEANS THAT JUST LIKE A BODY HAS MANY PARTS, PAPA GOD'S FAMILY, THE CHURCH, HAS MANY PARTS. YOU HAVE A SPECIAL PLACE OR PART IN HIS FAMILY, A ROLE THAT ONLY YOU CAN DO! IT'S KIND OF LIKE A TRUCK. A TRUCK HAS TO HAVE ALL OF ITS PARTS TO WORK THE RIGHT WAY, AND TO BE IN IT'S BEST CONDITION. IF PARTS WERE MISSING, LIKE AN ENGINE, IT WOULDN'T EVEN RUN! OR IF THE TRUCK HAD BROKEN WINDOWS OR A FLAT TIRE IT COULD BE DANGEROUS! OR WHAT IF A TRUCK HAD 3 STEERING WHEELS? THAT WOULD BE SILLY, YOU ONLY NEED ONE! PAPA GOD NEEDS HIS FAMILY TO WORK TOGETHER LIKE THE PARTS IN THIS TRUCK, TO BE IN THE BEST CONDITION THEY CAN BE, SO THEY CAN HELP DELIVER HIS KINGDOM TO EARTH.

THESE VEHICLES ARE MISSING PARTS! FINISH THE PICTURES. WHILE YOU ARE DRAWING, ASK, "HOLY SPIRIT, WHAT IS MY SPECIAL PART IN THE FAMILY? HOW DO I HELP DELIVER YOUR KINGDOM TO EARTH?"
WRITE OR DRAW WHAT HE SHARES ON THE DELIVERY TRUCK, THEN TELL HIM WHAT YOU THINK ABOUT YOUR PART!

ACTIVITY 5
FORGIVENESS

" Get rid of all bitterness, rage, anger, harsh words, and slander, as well as all types of evil behavior. Instead, be kind to each other, tenderhearted, forgiving one another, just as God through Christ has forgiven you."

EPHESIANS 4:31-32 NLT

HAS SOMEONE EVER DONE OR SAID SOMETHING THAT HURT YOUR HEART? HOW DID IT MAKE YOU FEEL? HAVE YOU EVER DONE OR SAID SOMETHING THAT HURT SOMEONE ELSE'S HEART? WHAT DO YOU USUALLY HAVE TO DO?...APOLOGIZE, AND SAY YOU'RE SORRY. DO YOU KNOW WHY WE DO THIS? BECAUSE FORGIVENESS IS VERY IMPORTANT! WHEN WE DON'T FORGIVE, OR ASK FOR FORGIVENESS, OUR HEARTS CAN'T BE WHOLE AND IT CAN FEEL LIKE A PIECE IS MISSING. IT'S OUR HEARTS THAT SUFFER WHEN WE DON'T FORGIVE OR APOLOGIZE - AND NOBODY WANTS A BROKEN HEART! ASK HOLY SPIRIT TO SHOW YOU IF THERE IS SOMEONE YOU NEED TO FORGIVE, EVEN IF THEY DIDN'T APOLOGIZE. SAY, "HOLY SPIRIT, IS THERE ANYONE I NEED TO FORGIVE THAT WILL FILL A MISSING PIECE IN MY HEART?" HAVE HOLY SPIRIT HELP YOU FORGIVE THEM BY TALKING TO HIM ABOUT THE HURT IN YOUR HEART, AND HOW IT MADE YOU FEEL. THEN, WHEN YOU ARE READY TO FORGIVE, FILL IN THE MISSING PIECES ON THE HEART.

Pray the words on the heart out loud, and use it as an example as often as you need to keep your heart whole!

I FORGIVE _____ FOR _____ AND HOW IT MADE ME FEEL _____.

DOESN'T YOUR HEART FEEL SO MUCH BETTER?! THAT'S BECAUSE IT'S WHOLE AGAIN! DECORATE THE WHOLE HEART AND CUT OUT THE PIECES. PUT IT BACK TOGETHER TO SHOW YOU THE IMPORTANCE OF NOT LETTING PIECES GO MISSING OR BEING BROKEN APART.

ACTIVITY
SECRET PLACE

"But whenever you pray, go into your innermost chamber and be alone with Father God, praying to him in secret..."

Matthew 6:6 TPT

Keep out
only Papa God allowed

How do you get to know someone? By spending time together! Papa God wants to spend time with just you! He is never too busy, and He never has better things to do. He always has time for you! So you can spend time with Him whenever you want! You can go to a special place to meet, or create a special place in your heart and mind to meet. This is called the secret place, where it is just you and Him. What can you do in your secret place? Anything you want!

You can talk to Him about your day, how you're feeling— like what makes you happy, or proud, or if something made you sad or angry. You can laugh, create, and play with Him. You can cry, listen, or just sit with Him. It's a great place to read His written word, the Bible, pray for others, sing, dance, and make memories together. It's all about creating a long lasting, true friendship!

Think of Papa God as your new BFF!

SPEND TIME MAKING A NEW MEMORY WITH PAPA GOD IN YOUR SECRET PLACE! DRAW OR WRITE WHAT YOUR SECRET PLACE LOOKS LIKE AND WHAT YOU DID TOGETHER TODAY.

CHALLENGE*

Go to your secret place everyday to continue to grow your friendship! * hint- Do it first thing in the morning for a great start, and then again at night before you go to sleep.

ACTIVITY

FLUSH THE LIES

"MY SON, PAY ATTENTION TO WHAT I SAY. LISTEN CLOSELY TO MY WORDS. DON'T LET THEM OUT OF YOUR SIGHT. NEVER STOP THINKING ABOUT THEM. THESE WORDS ARE THE SECRET OF LIFE AND HEALTH TO ALL WHO DISCOVER THEM. ABOVE ALL, BE CAREFUL WHAT YOU THINK BECAUSE YOUR THOUGHTS CONTROL YOUR LIFE."

Proverbs 4:20-23 ERV

What is something you spend a lot of time thinking about? What we think about is so important! Papa God tells us that we have to be CAREFUL what we think about, because our thoughts can control our lives. Here's an example: If all you ever thought was, "I can't do this," or "this is too hard," or "I'm not good enough," then you would miss out on trying and learning new things that Papa God has for you - and that would be awful! Our thoughts can take over what we do, how we feel, and how we act. Our thoughts can make our bodies healthy or they can make our bodies sick. Our thoughts can either be like taking vitamins or drinking poison!

Negative thoughts and lies can fill our minds and be like poison to our whole body. The more we have, the sicker we can get, because they are super toxic! Let's dump the toxic thoughts down the toilet and flush them away! Ask, "Holy Spirit, will you please show me the negative thoughts and lies that are toxic to me?" Write or draw your poisonous thoughts in the toilet bowl.

Positive thoughts, and Papa God's words, are like a multivitamin for our minds and bodies. They are packed full of everything our minds and bodies need to think and be healthy! Pop some vitamins of truth into your mind today! Ask, "Holy Spirit, will you give me some thoughts that are true?" Write or draw what you hear on the vitamins.

CHALLENGE*

Keep yourself healthy by taking your multivitamin of Papa God's truth EVERYDAY! Write His truths on paper, notecards, or your bathroom mirror (with permission) and think about them, read them, and speak them out loud!

ACTIVITY SUPERHERO — FEAR

"For God did not give us a spirit of fear, but of power and love and self control."

2 Timothy 1:7 ESV

HAVE YOU EVER FELT AFRAID? AFRAID OF SOMETHING? MAYBE YOU WERE NERVOUS, AND FEARFUL TO DO SOMETHING, TO SPEAK UP, OR OF WHAT SOMEONE MIGHT THINK? FEAR CAN LOOK LIKE DIFFERENT THINGS, BUT NONE OF THOSE THINGS COME FROM PAPA GOD. YOU ACTUALLY HAVE SUPER POWERS TO FIGHT FEAR! WHENEVER FEAR TRIES TO COME IN LIKE AN ENEMY, YOU HAVE EVERYTHING YOU NEED TO BE POWERFUL, TO BE LOVE, AND TO BE SELF-CONTROLLED. YOU CAN LOCK UP FEAR IN A CAGE, IN THE NAME OF JESUS, AND ASK HIM TO TAKE THE CAGE AWAY!

Think of the things that make you afraid. Create your own villain on the cards. Give them a name, a face, and describe how they make you afraid. Then you can recognize the villain and not let it escape! Now ask, "Holy Spirit, will you please show me how to defeat these villains?" Write on the card how He tells you to defeat them.

VILLAIN NAME

FEAR MISSION:

DEFEATED BY:

VILLAIN NAME

FEAR MISSION:

DEFEATED BY:

VILLAIN NAME

FEAR MISSION:

DEFEATED BY:

CHALLENGE*

If a fear-villain tries to escape and come back, or a new one comes to town, use your superpowers! Say out loud, wherever you are, "Fear, leave in the name of Jesus!" Be the superhero you were created to be!

ACTIVITY

JESUS IS OUR FRIEND

"No longer do I call you servants, for the servant does not know what his master is doing; but I have called you friends, for all that I have heard from my Father I have made known to you."

John 15:15 ESV

What do you like to do with your friends? Do you plan things? Play? Go on adventures? Jesus wants to do all of these things with you and more! And you can spend time with Him whenever you want. You don't have to wait for permission, or a "play date," just ask Him to join you in whatever you are doing. Wouldn't it be cool if you could spend everyday with your best friend? Well with Jesus you can! Brainstorm or draw a list of things you want to do with Jesus.

BONUS: NOW GO AND DO THEM TOGETHER!

Pick one or more things on your list and invite Jesus to go do them with you!

After you have done them, come back and write or draw about how much fun you had!

ACTIVITY 10

PALMS OF HIS HANDS

"See, I have written your name on the palm of my hands.."

Isaiah 49:16 NLT

Today we are going to quiet our minds, and our hearts, to focus on Papa God's great love for us. You are so special to Him! He sees you, knows you, and has even written, like a tattoo, YOUR NAME on the palms of His hands. You are always in his thoughts! Quiet your mind, close your eyes, and ask, "Jesus, will you show me what you have written on the palms of Your hands?" What do you see?
Write or draw what you see on the palms of His hands.

NOW, CLOSE YOUR EYES AGAIN, AND PICTURE JESUS SITTING IN A ROCKING CHAIR. HE JUST WANTS TO HOLD YOU TODAY. SPEND SOME TIME JUST LETTING HIM LOVE AND COMFORT YOU. TAKE YOUR TIME, AND ENJOY BEING STILL WITH YOUR PAPA. DRAW YOURSELF AND JESUS IN THE ROCKING CHAIR WHEN YOU ARE DONE!

ACTIVITY
CAST YOUR CARES

"Give all your worries and cares to God, for He cares about you."

1 PETER 5:7 NLT

Worries and cares are things that concern, bother, upset, or stress you out. If we keep all of our worries and cares to ourselves, it's like covering our hearts up with layers and layers of clothing. Each time you are worried or stressed about something you put another layer of clothing on top of your heart. If you put too many layers of clothing on you can begin to feel what? Well... think about being outside in a snowsuit during the summer. You would be very uncomfortable, it would be heavy, hot, you couldn't move well, and it would make you miserable and discouraged! This is what happens when we keep worrying and taking on stress that we don't need to put on. What does this verse say we need to do to get rid of those worries and cares? That's right! We just give it to Papa God, because He cares for you! He WANTS to take them, so you can be free to enjoy life.

ARE THERE ANY WORRIES, CARES, OR STRESSES THAT YOU HAVE BEEN LAYERING ON YOUR HEART? TAKE TIME TO WRITE THOSE THINGS ON THE PILE OF CLOTHES THAT JESUS IS HOLDING. EVERYTIME YOU WRITE ONE, SAY OUT LOUD "JESUS, I'M GIVING YOU_____! THANK YOU FOR TAKING IT AND HELPING ME!"

CHALLENGE:
When you start to feel those worries and cares layer up again, REMEMBER to just give them to JESUS!

ACTIVITY

"CALL ON PAPA GOD"

"The Lord watches over those who do what is right, and He listens to their prayers."

1 PETER 3:12 ERV

Have you ever tried calling someone and they didn't answer? They might be too busy, or they missed it, and that can be disappointing. BUT, do you know who will ALWAYS answer when you call?! That's right, Papa God! Not only will He answer, but He will listen, give advice, and be there to help you out when you need it.

Use the phones to text out your conversation to Papa God. Be sure to include your favorite emojis!

REMEMBER YOU CAN CALL ON HIM ANYTIME!

ACTIVITY

PRESCRIPTION OF JOY

"A joyful, cheerful heart brings healing to both body and soul. But the one whose heart is crushed struggles with sickness and depression."

PROVERBS 17:22 TPT

YOU CAN BE A DOCTOR! IF YOUR HEART IS EVER FEELING SAD OR SICK, IT NEEDS A PRESCRIPTION OF JOY! PAPA GOD CREATED YOUR HEART IN SUCH A WAY THAT IT CAN HEAL BY BEING JOYFUL.

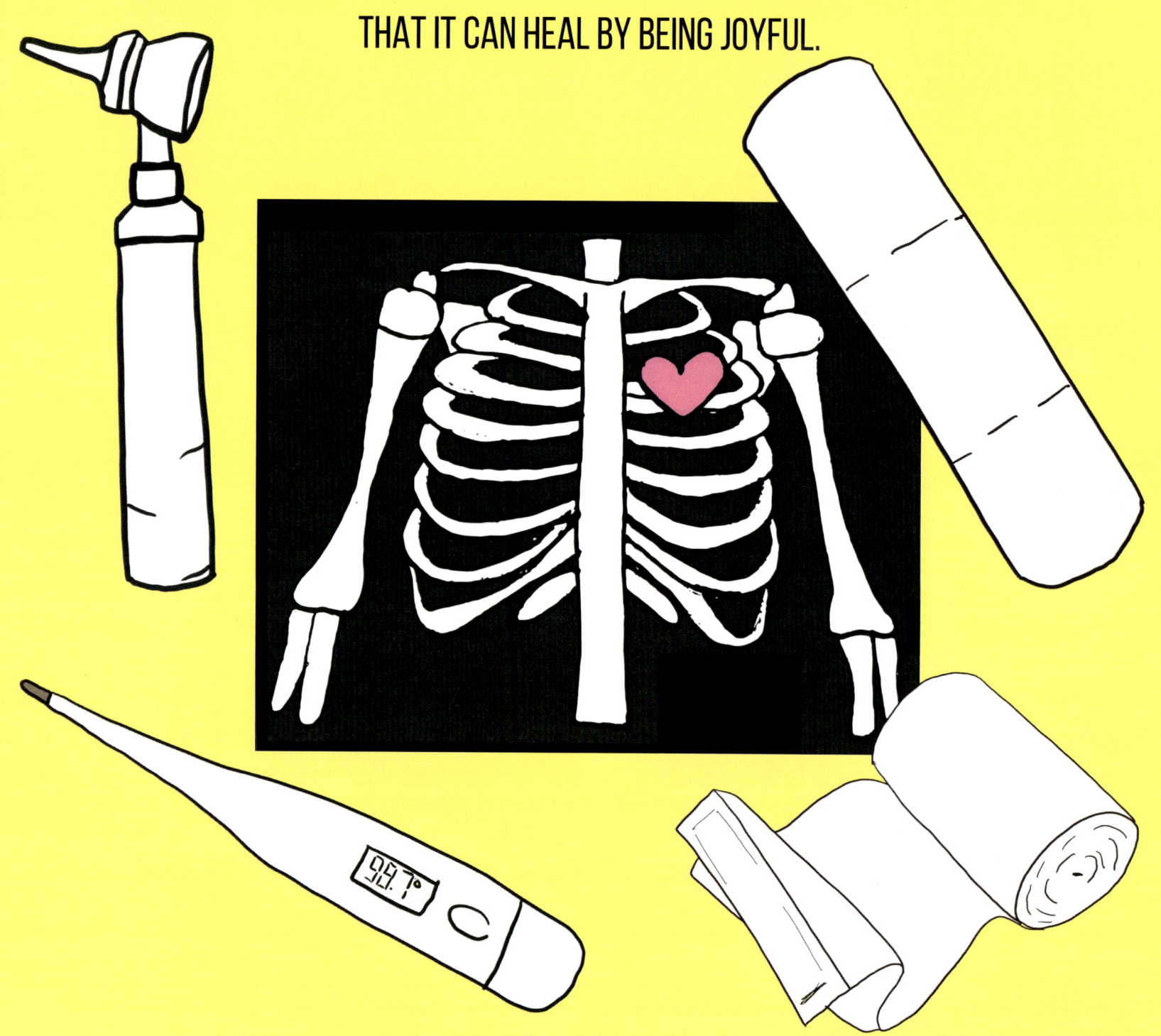

THINK OF ALL THE THINGS THAT YOU ENJOY. ASK, "HOLY SPIRIT, WILL YOU PLEASE SHOW ME ALL THE THINGS THAT BRING ME JOY?" WRITE ON ONE OF THE PRESCRIPTION PADS THE THINGS THAT GIVE YOU JOY FOR WHEN YOU NEED JOY MEDICINE. SPEND TIME WITH PAPA GOD THINKING ABOUT AND DOING THE THINGS THAT HE SHOWS YOU.

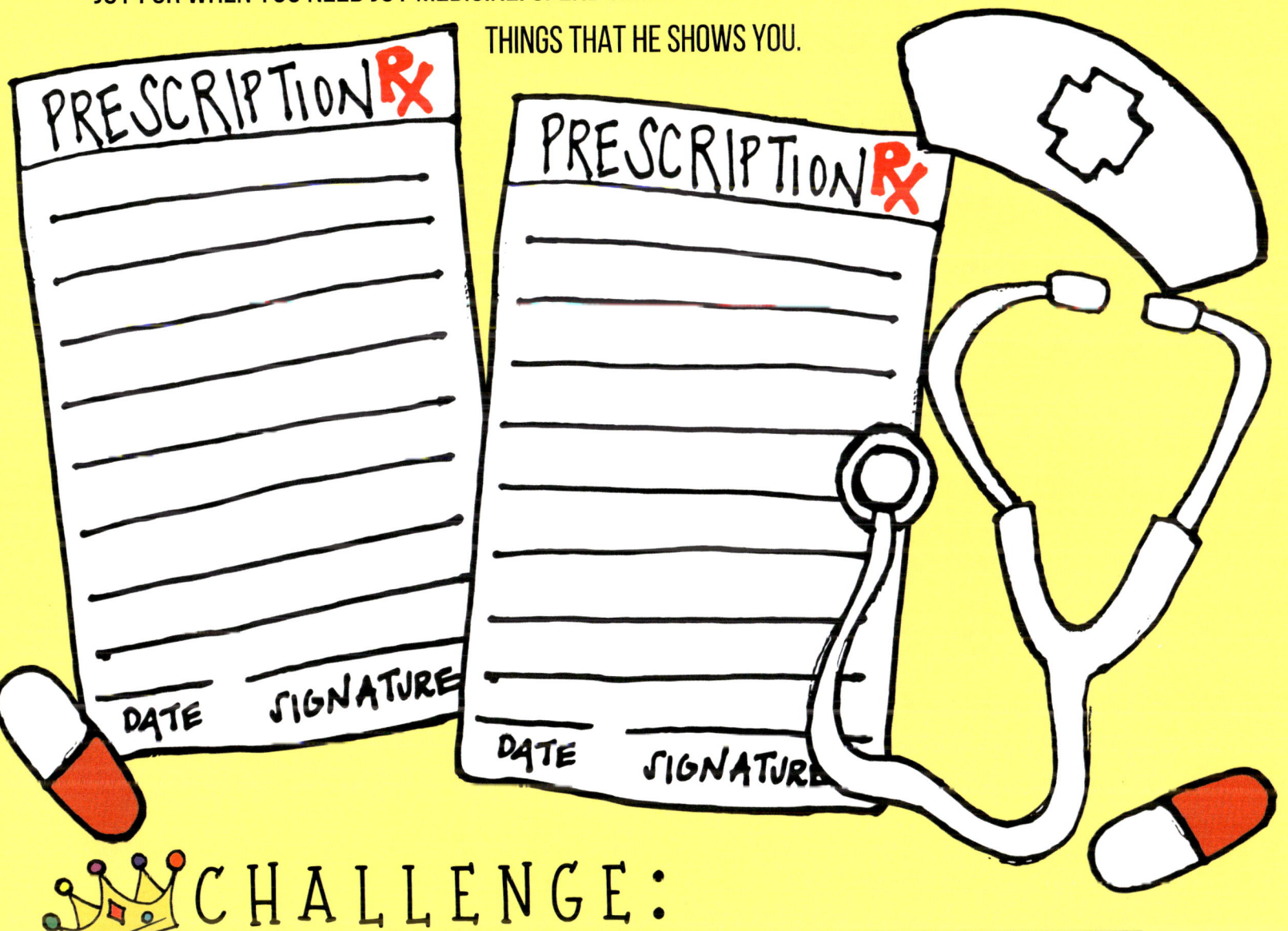

CHALLENGE:

ASK, "HOLY SPIRIT, WILL YOU SHOW ME SOMEONE THAT I CAN PRESCRIBE JOY MEDICINE TO, AND SHOW ME HOW I CAN GIVE THEM THEIR DOSE OF JOY?" WRITE WHAT HE SHOWS YOU ON THE SECOND PRESCRIPTION PAD.

NOW GO GIVE THEM THEIR DOSE OF JOY!

ACTIVITY 14

Words of Honey

"Kind words are like honey– sweet to the soul and healthy for the body."

PROVERBS 16:24 NLT

Throughout the day, people may say things that may hurt or sting your heart. It could be your brother or sister, a kid at school, or even a grownup. When this happens, it's usually because they are hurting and have been stung in their hearts. But this verse tells us that we have a choice. We can choose to sting them back with our words, or we can choose to speak kind words. When we choose to speak kind words, they are sweet, like honey, and they can heal the other person's heart and ours at the same time. Ask, "Holy Spirit, what are some kind words that can drip from my mouth like honey into someone's heart?" Write them on the heart below.

Now ask, "Holy Spirit, what are some words that have stung my heart that I need to forgive someone for saying?" Then ask, "what are some words that I have said that have stung someone else's heart that I need to apologize for, and replace with honey words?" Write them on the heart below and let Papa God heal them!

CHALLENGE:

PAPA GOD LOVES WHEN WE SPEAK SWEET, LIFE GIVING WORDS! LOOK IN HIS WORD, IN THE BOOK OF PROVERBS AND FIND 5 MORE EXAMPLES OF THE POWER OF OUR WORDS! HIGHLIGHT OR UNDERLINE THEM IN YOUR BIBLE.

ACTIVITY
MAKE A MELODY

"...Instead, be filled with the Holy Spirit, singing psalms and hymns and spiritual songs among yourselves, and making music to the Lord in your hearts."

EPHESIANS 5:18-19 NLT

ARE YOU READY TO HAVE SOME FUN TODAY? THE HOLY SPIRIT CAN FILL US SO FULL THAT OUR HEARTS OVERFLOW WITH JOYFUL SONGS TO PAPA GOD. SAY, "HOLY SPIRIT, COME FILL ME UP WITH PAPA GOD'S JOY AND LOVE." NOW, LET SONGS AND MUSIC BURST OUT OF YOUR HEART. SING OUT WHATEVER COMES TO MIND! JUST HAVE FUN PRAISING PAPA GOD TODAY!

ON THE SHEET OF MUSIC, WRITE THE WORDS AND DRAW THE NOTES TO YOUR NEW SONG! BONUS: CREATE YOUR OWN INSTRUMENT TO PRAISE THE LORD!

CHALLENGE:

TURN ON SOME WORSHIP MUSIC AND SING AND DANCE IN HIS PRESENCE.

ACTIVITY 16

I AM WITH YOU

"...DON'T BE AFRAID. I SAVED YOU. I NAMED YOU. YOU ARE MINE. WHEN YOU HAVE TROUBLES, I AM WITH YOU. WHEN YOU CROSS RIVERS, YOU WILL NOT BE HURT. WHEN YOU WALK THROUGH FIRE, YOU WILL NOT BE BURNED; THE FLAMES WILL NOT HURT YOU. THAT'S BECAUSE I, THE LORD, AM YOUR GOD. I, THE HOLY ONE OF ISRAEL, AM YOUR SAVIOR..."

ISAIAH 43:1-3 ERV

We can't always control our circumstances, but we can control how we handle those circumstances. Sometimes life can leave us feeling like we are alone, drowning, in a fire, or going through an impossible situation with no way out. But the good news is that we are NEVER alone. We don't have to let those disasters overwhelm us because Papa God is walking through them with us. We are HIS!

Think about a time when you felt like you were going through a disaster, or maybe you're going through one right now. Close your eyes and ask, "Holy Spirit, will You take me to a disaster in my life? And, will You take me there without feeling any of the pain?" When you are in the memory ask, "Holy Spirit, will You show me where Jesus was during this disaster?" Draw or write what you saw, heard, or felt.

ACTIVITY 17

ARMOR OF PAPA GOD

"Therefore, put on every piece of God's armor so you will be able to resist the enemy in the time of evil. Then after the battle you will still be standing firm. Stand your ground, putting on the belt of truth and the body armor of God's righteousness. For shoes, put on the peace that comes from the Good News so that you will be fully prepared. In addition to all of these, hold up the shield of faith to stop the fiery arrows of the devil. Put on salvation as your helmet, and take the sword of the Spirit, which is the word of God."

EPHESIANS 6:13-17 NLT

Until we go home to Heaven, we have a real battle we are in everyday. Satan, Papa God's enemy, is our enemy too. He tries to attack us by: lying to our minds, by using other people's actions towards us, or tempting us to sin. BUT! We have a FULL suit of armor that Papa God designed for us to wear. We can put it on everyday to protect ourselves from the attacks.

Go back through the verses and highlight or underline all the different pieces of armor. Label and color the pieces of armor. Say, "Holy Spirit, will you please show me what this piece of armor is protecting?" Write down what He shows you under each piece of armor. Then, put on your armor by imagining to grab each piece and placing it on your body where it should go.

Say out loud what piece you are putting on and what it protects you from.

FOR EXAMPLE, "I AM PUTTING ON MY HELMET, AND IT PROTECTS ME FROM THE LIES OF THE ENEMY!"

CHALLENGE:

PUT ON YOUR ARMOR EVERYDAY! FIND MATERIALS TO CREATE A PIECE OF ARMOR, OR THE WHOLE SET AS A REMINDER!

ACTIVITY

SUPER DETECTIVE

"I won't set my eyes on anything worthless. I hate wrongdoing; none of that will stick to me."

PSALM 101:3 CEB

Your eyes are one way you receive information into your mind and heart. Whether it be on a phone, tv show, video game, magazine, book, or movie - it all gets downloaded into your brain. Wow! What are you letting yourself see? Remember how thoughts can be toxic like poison? The things you see can create images and thoughts that can become poisonous. Papa God wants you to be aware of the things you see because there are things you were never supposed to see. These things are not a part of who Papa God is, and how you were made to live. Like any good parent, He only wants the BEST for you! Papa God wants to help you be a detective by showing you how to spot the clues that lead to destruction.

Draw the footprints as you walk to each clue.

VIOLENCE

LANGUAGE

ADULT CONTENT

!

STOP

WARNING!

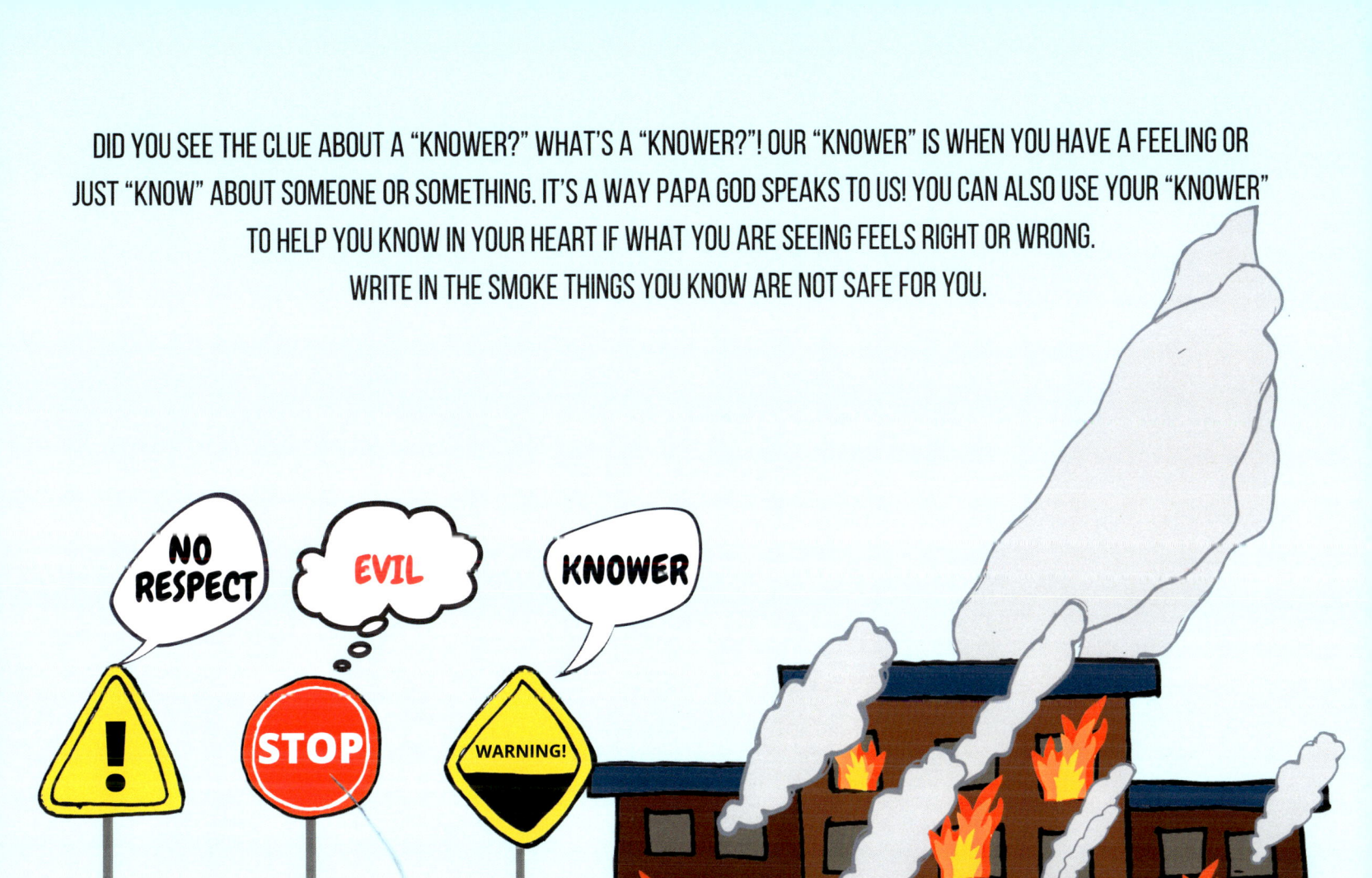

DID YOU SEE THE CLUE ABOUT A "KNOWER?" WHAT'S A "KNOWER?"! OUR "KNOWER" IS WHEN YOU HAVE A FEELING OR JUST "KNOW" ABOUT SOMEONE OR SOMETHING. IT'S A WAY PAPA GOD SPEAKS TO US! YOU CAN ALSO USE YOUR "KNOWER" TO HELP YOU KNOW IN YOUR HEART IF WHAT YOU ARE SEEING FEELS RIGHT OR WRONG. WRITE IN THE SMOKE THINGS YOU KNOW ARE NOT SAFE FOR YOU.

CHALLENGE:

Now that you can be a super detective with Papa God, think about the things that you choose to look at. Use your "knower" and the warning signs to solve whether or not you should be letting your eyes see what they see.

ACTIVITY

TICKING TIME BOMB

"My dearest brothers and sisters, take this to heart: Be quick to listen, but slow to speak. And be slow to become angry."

JAMES 1:19 TPT

Think about something that makes you really angry. What happens with your body and your words...do you EXPLODE?! Anger can be like a bomb ready to explode if you don't diffuse it quickly. And just like a bomb, anger can hurt those it hits. Write on the bombs things that make you feel angry.
Write on the explosions things that make you feel angry.

It's okay to feel angry, but it's not okay to explode at others. We can keep our bombs from exploding by being slow to speak, quick to listen, and patient. Say,
"Holy Spirit, will You please take how I handle my anger, and show me ways
I can be patient in the times I want to explode?" Write or draw what He shows you on the clock.

CHALLENGE:
THE VERSE ALSO TALKS ABOUT BEING SLOW TO SPEAK, AND BEING A GOOD LISTENER. ASK, "HOLY SPIRIT, WHY IS IT IMPORTANT THAT I AM SLOW TO SPEAK AND THAT I LISTEN WELL? HOW DOES THAT HELP ME AND OTHERS?"

ACTIVITY

EVERY GOOD GIFT

"Everything good comes from God. Every perfect gift is from him. These good gifts come down from the Father who made all the lights in the sky. But God never changes like the shadows from those lights. He is always the same."

James 1:17 ERV

Bad things can happen in our lives, and the enemy likes to trick us into thinking that Papa God is not good. But this verse tells us that "everything good comes from Papa God." God is good, there is no shadow of darkness in Him and He never changes. The more we get to know Him, the more we know His goodness. Spend time thinking about the good things in your life. If it's good, it came from Papa God! Write the good things He's given you on the gifts. Finish the drawing, and add more gifts He shows you.

NOW TELL PAPA GOD HOW MUCH THOSE GIFTS MEAN TO YOU BY WRITING HIM THANK YOU NOTES!

ACTIVITY
CARRY YOUR MIRACLE

"As Jesus sat down, he looked out and saw the massive crowd of people scrambling up the hill, for they wanted to be near him. So he turned to Philip and said, "Where will we buy enough food to feed all these people?" Now Jesus already knew what he was about to do, but he said this to stretch Philip's faith. Philip answered, "Well, I suppose if we were to give everyone only a snack, it would cost thousands of dollars to buy enough food!" But just then, Andrew, Peter's brother, spoke up and said, "Look! Here's a young person with five barley loaves and two small fish . . . but how far would that go with this huge crowd?" "Have everyone sit down," Jesus said to his disciples. So on the vast grassy slope, more than five thousand hungry people sat down. Jesus then took the barley loaves [E] and the fish and gave thanks to God. He then gave it to the disciples to distribute to the people. Miraculously, the food multiplied, with everyone eating as much as they wanted! When everyone was satisfied, Jesus told his disciples, "Now go back and gather up the pieces left over so that nothing will be wasted." The disciples filled up twelve baskets of fragments, a basket of leftovers for each disciple. All the people were astounded as they saw with their own eyes the incredible miracle Jesus had performed! They began to say among themselves, "He really is the one—the true prophet we've been expecting!""

JOHN 6:5-14 TPT

What an amazing miracle story! Did you catch that Jesus fed thousands of people with only 5 loaves and 2 fish? He prayed to His Papa God and the food was MULTIPLIED! The people had all they could eat, and still had 12 baskets left over! Papa God is still doing miracles today, and he wants YOU to be a part of them. Did you also catch who gave the disciples the food? A young person, a child, like you! All the child did was offer Jesus what he had, and Jesus used it to bless thousands. The child could have thought, "I don't have near enough, I won't even try," but he didn't, he gave what he had. This story also tells us that Jesus knew what was going to happen, He was just waiting for the child to come. He just wants YOU! What do you have that you can give to Jesus? Maybe you aren't sure, but Papa God knows what you have, just like Jesus did with the child. Ask Him, "Jesus, what do I have that You can use to bless others in Your Kingdom?"

WRITE OR DRAW WHAT YOU CAN GIVE – IN, AND AROUND THE LUNCH BOX.

CHALLENGE:
Papa God loves your generous heart! Take time to pray for what you have to give. Hold out your hands like you're giving, and pray "Papa God, I thank you for _____ (what you're giving). I trust and believe that You will do great things with what I can give! I'm excited to see Your miracle works! I love You Papa God! In Jesus name, amen!"

ACTIVITY
TIGHT ROPE

"So we are always confident, even though we know that as long as we live in these bodies we are not at home with the Lord. For we live by believing and not by seeing."

2 CORINTHIANS 5:6-7 NLT

Sometimes trusting in Papa God and the plans He has for our lives can seem scary. If we don't see an answer to prayer, or if life doesn't look like what we think it should look like, or if He asks us to do something that seems risky (example: asking the mean kid to be your friend), it can be hard to trust Him. It's kind of like walking on a tightrope with a blindfold on. Papa God asks us to step out in faith, even when we can't see, and believe that He will keep us safe, and has a great
reward for us on the other side.

Ask Him, "Holy Spirit, will You show me a risk You're asking me to take to trust You more?" Write or draw on the opposite cliff, what He shows you and what you are believing for. Spend time talking with Papa God about how all of this makes you feel, and then draw yourself on the tightrope walking towards Jesus as you trust Him with your heart.

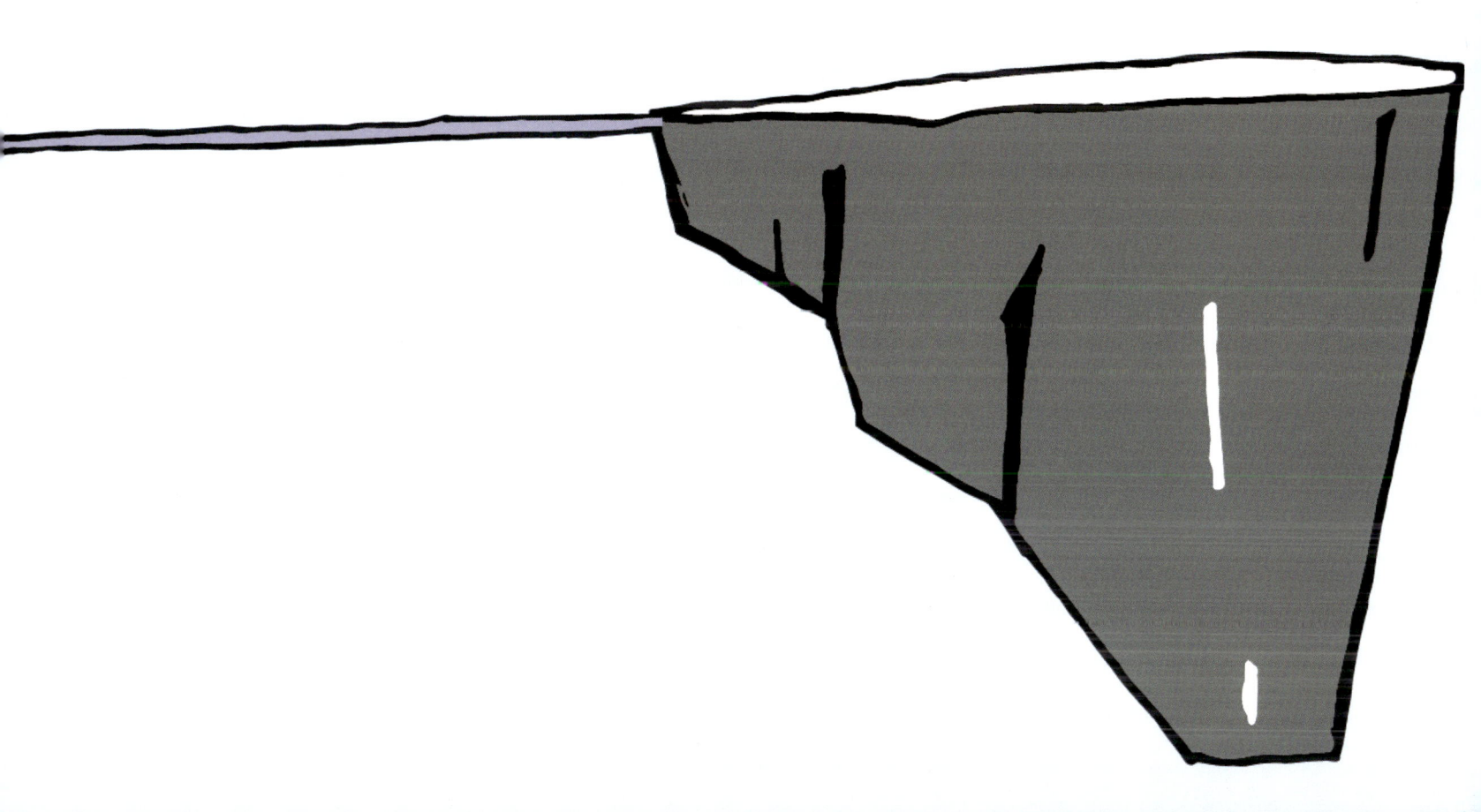

ACTIVITY

MAP OF INTERCESSION

"First of all, I ask that you pray for all people. Ask God to bless them and give them what they need. And give thanks. You should pray for rulers and for all who have authority. Pray for these leaders so that we can live quiet and peaceful lives—lives full of devotion to God and respect for him. This is good and pleases God our Savior. God wants everyone to be saved and to fully understand the truth."

1 TIMOTHY 2:1-4 ERV

AS PART OF PAPA GOD'S FAMILY, HE WANTS US TO PRAY FOR THE OTHER MEMBERS OF HIS FAMILY, AND FOR PEOPLE TO KNOW THEY CAN COME TO HIS FAMILY, ALL OVER THE WORLD!

Europe

North America

Atlantic Ocean

Pacific Ocean

South America

Antartica

LOOK AT THIS MAP. PRAY AND ASK, "HOLY SPIRIT, PLEASE SHOW ME A NATION." NOW, CIRCLE IT. ASK HIM, "HOW CAN I PRAY FOR THIS NATION, AND HOW CAN HEAVEN BE RELEASED IN THAT PLACE? WHAT IS YOUR HEART FOR YOUR PEOPLE THERE?" WRITE OR DRAW WHAT HE SHOWS YOU. THE MORE YOU PRAY FOR SOMETHING OR SOMEONE, THE MORE YOUR HEART STARTS TO CARE FOR THEM. YOUR PRAYERS ARE MORE POWERFUL THAN YOU WILL EVER KNOW! PLACE YOUR HAND ON THE NATION AND PRAY FOR IT OFTEN!

Arctic Ocean

Europe

Asia

Africa

Pacific Ocean

Indian Ocean

Australia

CHALLENGE:

Ask, "Holy Spirit, please show me more about this nation. Is there a specific city or need?" There are ways you can find out about different countries. For example, books, the library, or the internet.

ACTIVITY
DREAMS

"Then he (Joseph) had another dream, and he told it to his brothers. "Listen," he said, "I had another dream, and this time the sun and moon and eleven stars were bowing down to me."

GENESIS 37:9 NIV

All throughout the Bible, Papa God speaks to people in dreams – this is one of the ways He still speaks to us today. Dreams can happen while you sleep, or while you are awake. A dream can also be a desire in your heart. In this story, Joseph was given a dream about his future and it came true! Sometimes we don't always know what our dreams mean, but we can ask Papa God to tell us directly, or we can ask someone who we trust and love to tell us what our dreams mean.

Nightmares are NOT from Papa God. IF you have nightmares, say out loud, "in the name of Jesus, nightmares go! Papa God, protect my mind and give me peaceful dreams from You."

If you remember a dream you've had, spend time talking with Papa God about it. Then spend time dreaming with Him about your future. Write or draw what He is showing you in the dream bubbles.

CHALLENGE:

WHEN YOU GO TO SLEEP, PRAY, "PAPA GOD, PLEASE PROTECT MY HEART AND MY MIND TONIGHT AND GIVE ME BEAUTIFUL DREAMS FROM YOU." MAKE SURE TO WRITE DOWN OR DRAW WHAT YOU DREAM SO THAT YOU CAN REMEMBER AND REFLECT.

ACTIVITY
AUDIENCE OF ONE

"For am I now seeking the approval of man, or of God? Or am I trying to please man? If I were still trying to please man, I would not be a servant of Christ."

GALATIANS 1:10 ESV

Do you ever care about what people might think about you? For example, will people like me? Or what do they think of my ideas? What about when you do things because you love Papa God? Have you ever wanted to raise your hands or dance during worship? Or start a bible study at your school? Or go pray for someone, but you didn't because you were afraid of what others would think? This can be called "fear of man". This verse says we should care more about what Papa God thinks than what people think. Papa God's approval is all that matters and He approves of you big time!

Think of it like a stage and you have His full attention all the time! He loves watching you do what He created you to do. Ask, "Holy Spirit, will you please show me what I would be doing if I didn't let the thoughts of others hold me back?"

Draw or write what He tells you on the stage.

ACTIVITY

WONDERFULLY MADE

"You formed the way I think and feel. You put me together in my mother's womb. I praise you because you made me in such a wonderful way. I know how amazing that was! You could see my bones grow as my body took shape, hidden in my mother's womb. You could see my body grow each passing day. You listed all my parts, and not one of them was missing."

Psalms 139:13-15 ERV

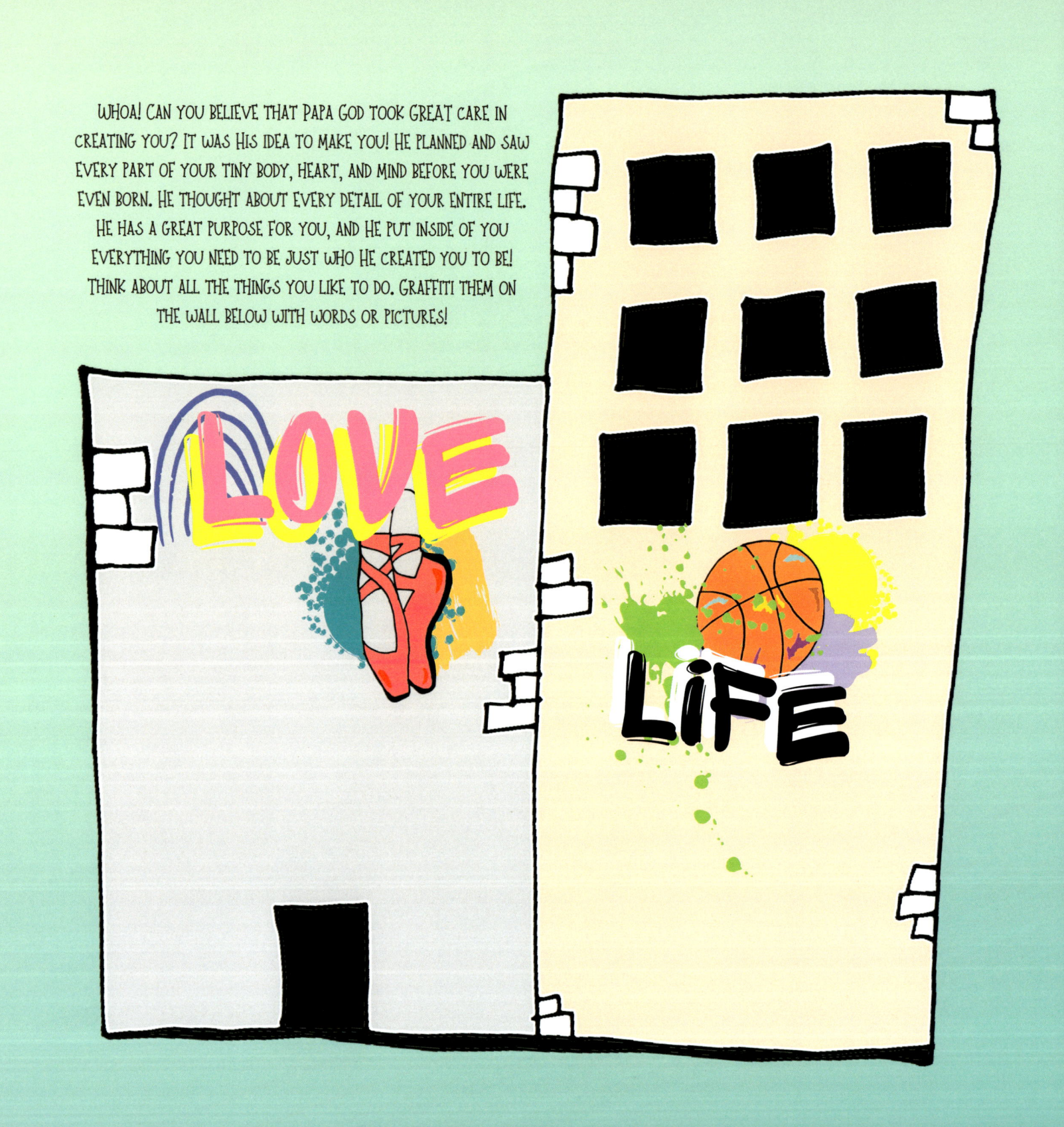

Whoa! Can you believe that Papa God took great care in creating you? It was His idea to make you! He planned and saw every part of your tiny body, heart, and mind before you were even born. He thought about every detail of your entire life. He has a great purpose for you, and He put inside of you everything you need to be just who He created you to be! Think about all the things you like to do. Graffiti them on the wall below with words or pictures!

LOVE

LIFE

YOU DON'T LIKE THINGS JUST BECAUSE...YOU ARE DRAWN TO THOSE THINGS BECAUSE THEY ARE PART OF THE WAY PAPA GOD MADE YOU UNIQUE. PICK 3 OF YOUR FAVORITE THINGS AND ASK, "HOLY SPIRIT, WILL YOU PLEASE SHOW ME WHY YOU GAVE ME MY DESIRES, HOW I CAN USE THEM TO BE WHO YOU CREATED ME TO BE, AND HOW THEY CAN BLESS OTHERS?"
WRITE WHAT HE TELLS YOU ON THE WALL NEXT TO THE NUMBERS!

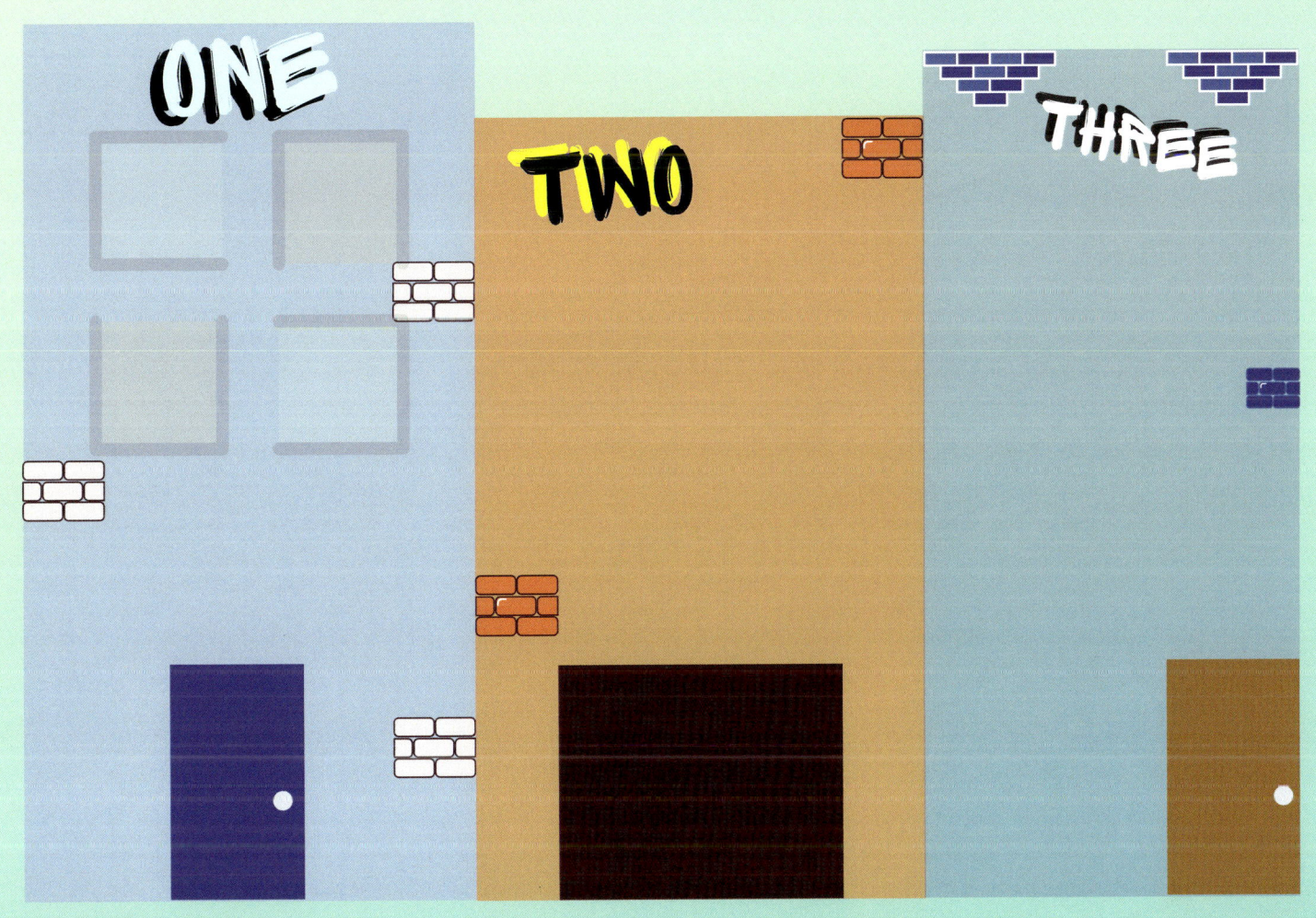

ONE

TWO

THREE

👑 CHALLENGE

KEEP BEING YOU! KEEP DOING THESE THINGS WITH PAPA GOD AND HE WILL CONTINUE TO SHOW YOU MORE AND MORE HOW THESE ARE A PART OF YOU AND HOW TO USE THEM! REMEMBER- DON'T LET THE ENEMY POISON YOUR THOUGHTS THROUGH LIES, OR OTHER PEOPLE'S NEGATIVE OPINIONS. YOU BE YOU!

ACTIVITY 27
DECLARATIONS

"Then the Lord reached out and touched my mouth and said, "Look, I have put my words in your mouth!"

JEREMIAH 1:9 NLT

Papa God loves it when we say His words over ourselves. These can be called affirmations. The more we speak Papa God's words over ourselves, the more we become like Him. Let's practice!

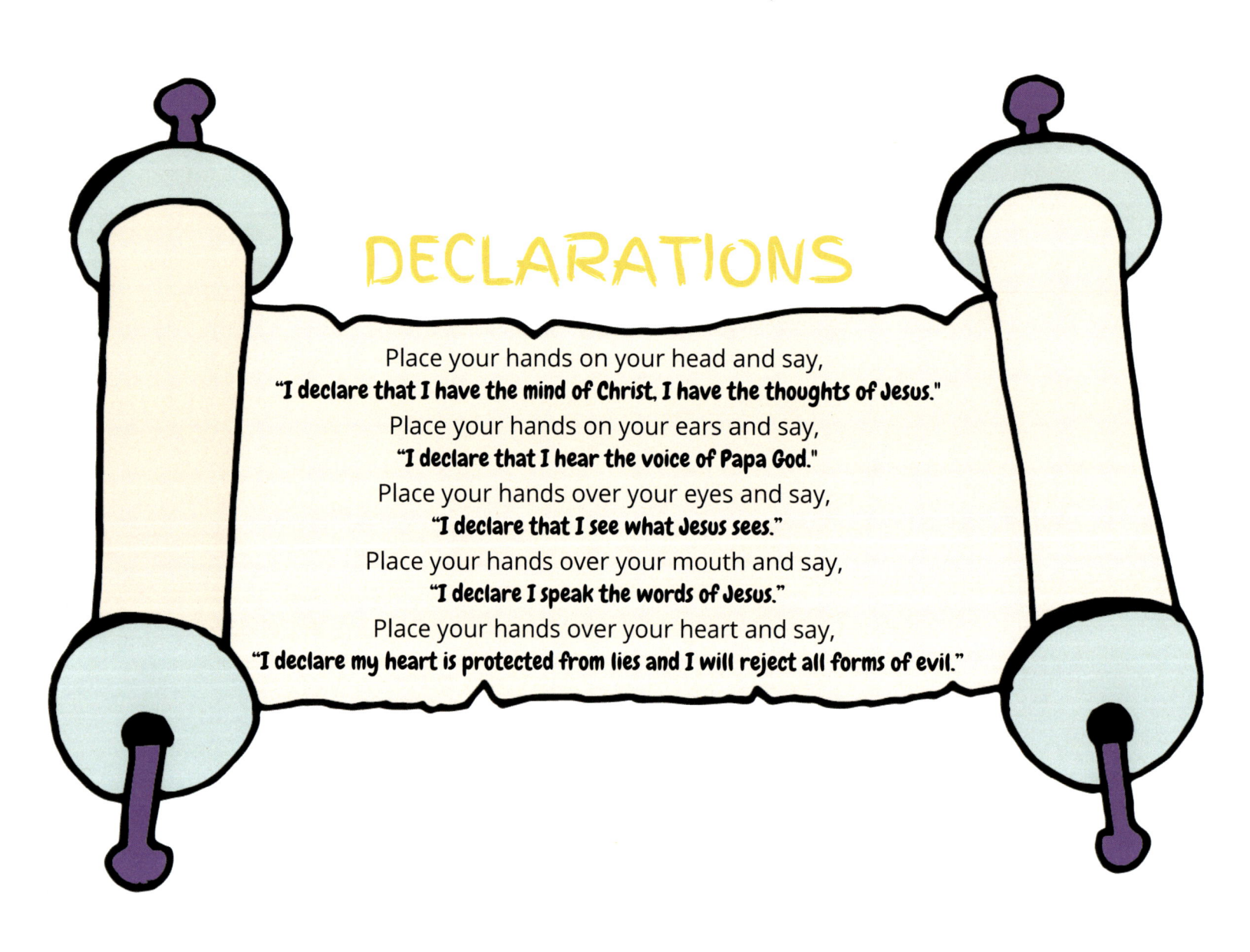

DECLARATIONS

Place your hands on your head and say,
"I declare that I have the mind of Christ, I have the thoughts of Jesus."

Place your hands on your ears and say,
"I declare that I hear the voice of Papa God."

Place your hands over your eyes and say,
"I declare that I see what Jesus sees."

Place your hands over your mouth and say,
"I declare I speak the words of Jesus."

Place your hands over your heart and say,
"I declare my heart is protected from lies and I will reject all forms of evil."

Finish drawing the person to look like you!

CHALLENGE:

SAY THIS OUTLOUD EVERYDAY! YOU CAN ADD NEW DECLARATIONS EACH DAY BASED ON WHAT THE HOLY SPIRIT IS TELLING YOU. EXAMPLE: "I HAVE A HEART OF COMPASSION AND UNCONDITIONAL LOVE!"

ACTIVITY
RECIPE OF LOVE

"LOVE IS PATIENT AND KIND. LOVE IS NOT JEALOUS, IT DOES NOT BRAG, AND IT IS NOT PROUD. LOVE IS NOT RUDE, IT IS NOT SELFISH, AND IT CANNOT BE MADE ANGRY EASILY. LOVE DOES NOT REMEMBER WRONGS DONE AGAINST IT. LOVE IS NEVER HAPPY WHEN OTHERS DO WRONG, BUT IT IS ALWAYS HAPPY WITH THE TRUTH. LOVE NEVER GIVES UP ON PEOPLE. IT NEVER STOPS TRUSTING, NEVER LOSES HOPE, AND NEVER QUITS. LOVE WILL NEVER END..."

1 CORINTHIANS 13:4-8 ERV

We all want to be loved and to give love! Think of all the people you love and who love you back. Love feels good right? But sometimes, there are people in our lives that don't show us the right kind of love, and that hurts Papa God's heart. The love from people doesn't even come close to Papa God's love for us! His love is perfect and unconditional, in fact, Papa God IS LOVE! He has given us a recipe for what love should look like, feel like, and taste like!

Read over the love verse again. Cross off all the ingredients that love is NOT. Then write on the ingredients what love IS.

- angry
- selfish
- rude
- bragging
- proud
- jealous

Write a love letter on the recipe card for someone that you love, or someone that needs to be loved.

Recipe _____

CHALLENGE:

Invite Papa God to make your favorite recipe with you. Pray Papa God's love into it as you make it! Cut out the recipe card and take it and your goodies to the person He showed you!

ACTIVITY

TEACHER HOLY SPIRIT

"But the Helper will teach you everything and cause you to remember all that I told you. This Helper is the Holy Spirit that the Father will send in my name."

JOHN 14:26 ERV

Remember when you asked Jesus to come live in your heart and set you free? When you did that, Papa God sent His Holy Spirit to come live inside of you! The Holy Spirit is His gift to us so that we can always have access to Papa God and stay connected to His heart. The Holy Spirit has many different roles or ways He helps us. Look over the list of roles and spend time talking to the Holy Spirit about how He can be those for you.

For example, "Holy Spirit, how can you be my comforter?"

RESUME for Holy Spirit

ROLES
- ✓ COMFORTER
- ✓ COUNSELOR
- ✓ ADVOCATE
- ✓ ENCOURAGER
- ✓ INTERCESSOR
- ✓ HELPER
- ✓ FRIEND
- ✓ TEACHER

Today, Papa God wants you to get to know the Holy Spirit as your teacher. He can teach us things from Papa God's word that maybe we didn't see or understand before. Ask, "Holy Spirit, will you show me verses, or a story in the Bible that Papa God wants me to read?" Then, after you read it, ask, "Holy Spirit, what do you want me to learn from this?" Write or draw on the chalkboard what you learned. Try these out if you need help starting!

1 Samuel 17,   Daniel 6,   Luke 10:38-42,   Psalm 34

ACTIVITY
TESTIMONY

"He (Jesus) said, "Go home to your family and friends. Tell them about all that the Lord did for you. Tell them how the Lord was good to you." So the man left and told the people in the Ten Towns about the great things Jesus did for him. Everyone was amazed."

MARK 5:19-20 ERV

A testimony is sharing your story of what Papa God has done for you. The man in this story had been set free and healed by Jesus. He was so excited he ran and told his friends and everyone what Jesus had done! Because of his story, many others believed in Jesus and became part of the family of Papa God. We get to share our story too!

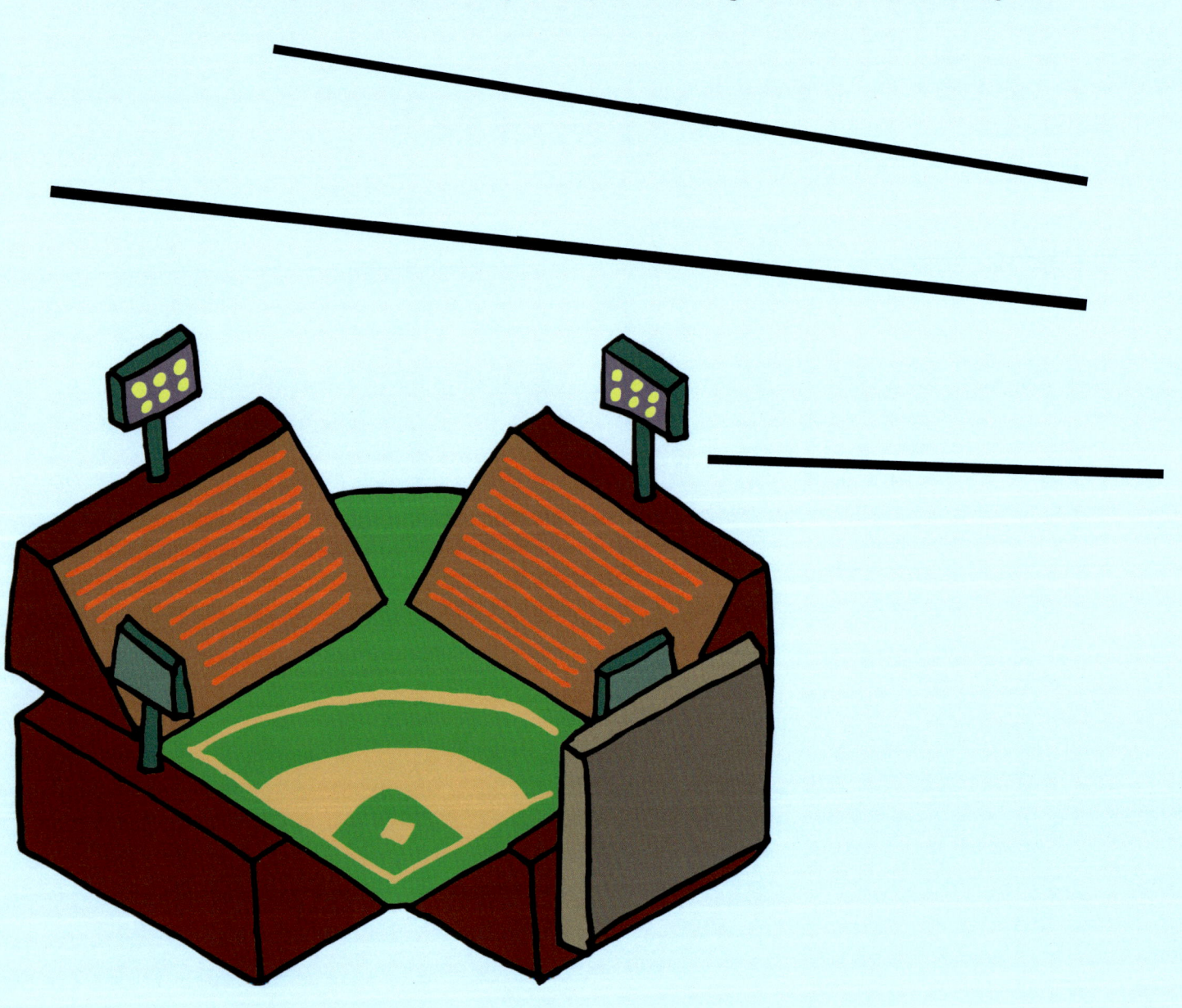

Spend time talking with Papa God about your story and how He has changed your life. Say, "Holy Spirit, what should people know about what You've done in my life that could change their lives too?" Write what He tells you coming out of the mega phone.

ACTIVITY BLUEPRINTS

"You will find true success when you find me, for I have insight into wise plans that are designed just for you. I hold in my hands living-understanding, courage, and strength."

PROVERBS 8:14 TPT

Papa God is so proud of all the work you have done with Him in this book! You have let Him into your heart, and He has begun to show you who you were created to be! But your purpose doesn't stop here, it's just the beginning of the plans He is showing you for your life. Papa God has a special set of blueprints (plans) that He has designed uniquely just for YOU! You are the only one who has this specific set of blueprints planned out for you. As you grow with Papa God, He will reveal more of your blueprint and it will be awesome to see how it all fits together!

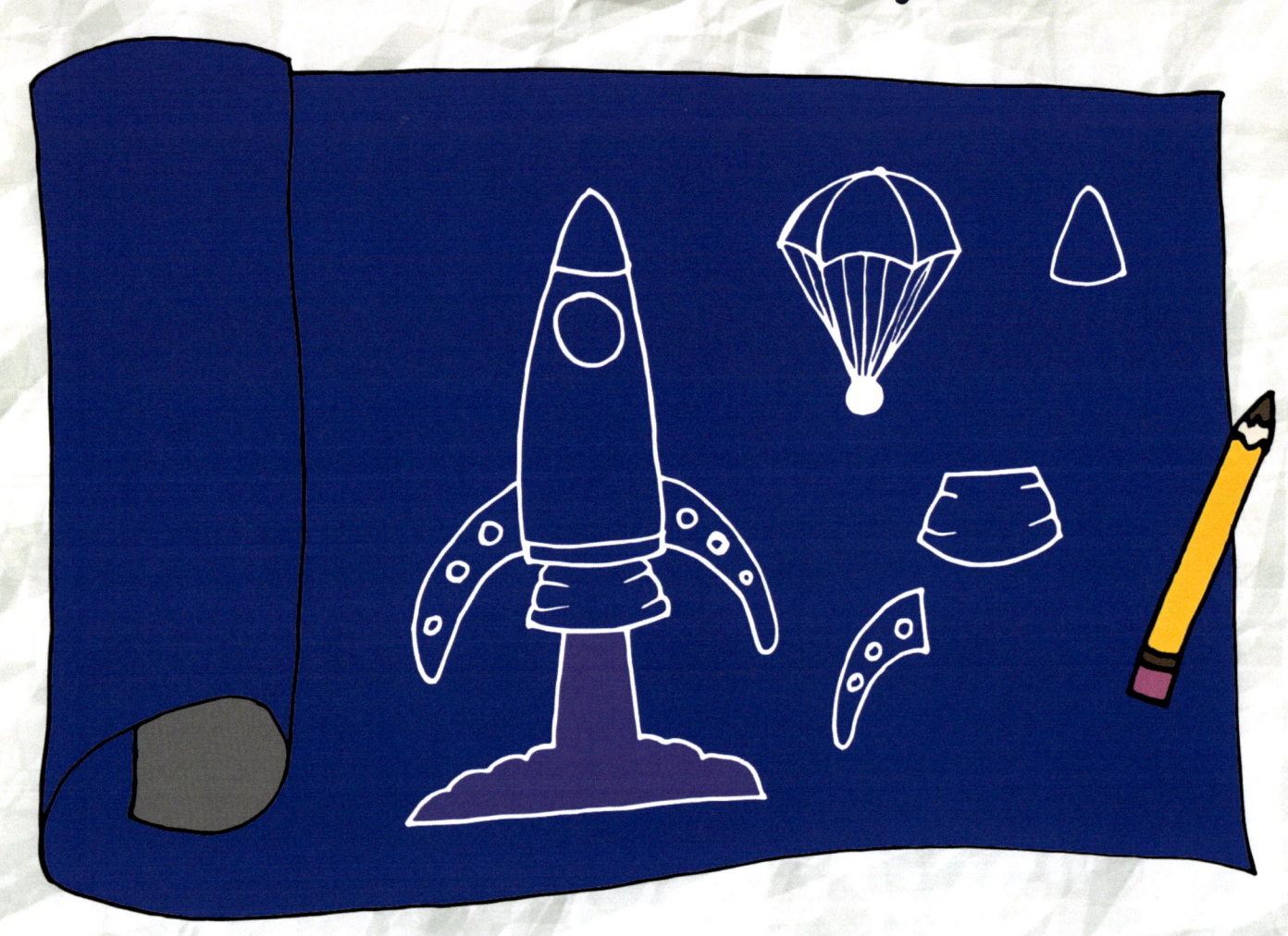

Ask, "Holy Spirit, will You please be my pen and come draw more details of my life on this blueprint?"

CHALLENGE:

Remember, as you let Papa God show you more of the design He has for YOUR life, all of His blueprints are drawn with LOVE. In everything you do, the most important thing is to do it with HIS love. If you are loving, then you are in the right design. So LOVE BIG!